SECOND EDITION

TOUCHSTONE

WORKBOOK 2A

T0159688

MICHAEL MCCARTHY
JEANNE MCCARTEN
HELEN SANDIFORD

CAMBRIDGE
UNIVERSITY PRESS

CAMBRIDGE
UNIVERSITY PRESS & ASSESSMENT

Shaftesbury Road, Cambridge CB2 8EA, United Kingdom

One Liberty Plaza, 20th Floor, New York, NY 10006, USA

477 Williamstown Road, Port Melbourne, VIC 3207, Australia

314–321, 3rd Floor, Plot 3, Splendor Forum, Jasola District Centre, New Delhi – 110025, India

103 Penang Road, #05-06/07, Visioncrest Commercial, Singapore 238467

Cambridge University Press & Assessment is a department of the University of Cambridge.

We share the University's mission to contribute to society through the pursuit of education, learning and research at the highest international levels of excellence.

www.cambridge.org
Information on this title: www.cambridge.org/9781107649880

© Cambridge University Press & Assessment 2005, 2014

This publication is in copyright. Subject to statutory exception and to the provisions of relevant collective licensing agreements, no reproduction of any part may take place without the written permission of Cambridge University Press & Assessment.

First published 2005
Second Edition 2014

20 19 18 17 16 15 14 13 12 11

Printed in Great Britain by Ashford Colour Press Ltd.

A catalog record for this publication is available from the British Library.

ISBN 978-1-107-68173-6 Student's Book
ISBN 978-1-107-68175-0 Student's Book A
ISBN 978-1-107-62704-8 Student's Book B
ISBN 978-1-107-69037-0 Workbook
ISBN 978-1-107-64988-0 Workbook A
ISBN 978-1-107-61861-9 Workbook B
ISBN 978-1-107-65940-7 Full Contact
ISBN 978-1-107-61439-0 Full Contact A
ISBN 978-1-107-66547-7 Full Contact B
ISBN 978-1-107-62402-3 Teacher's Edition with Assessment Audio CD/CD-ROM
ISBN 978-1-107-67757-9 Class Audio CDs (4)

Additional resources for this publication at www.cambridge.org/touchstone2

Cambridge University Press & Assessment has no responsibility for the persistence or accuracy of URLs for external or third-party internet websites referred to in this publication, and does not guarantee that any content on such websites is, or will remain, accurate or appropriate. Information regarding prices, travel timetables, and other factual information given in this work is correct at the time of first printing but Cambridge University Press & Assessment does not guarantee the accuracy of such information thereafter.

Contents

1 Making friends 2
2 Interests 10
3 Health 18
4 Celebrations 26
5 Growing up 34
6 Around town 42

Making friends

UNIT 1

Lesson A Getting to know you

1 About you 1

Grammar and vocabulary **A** **Complete the chart with the words in the box.**

college	major	✓neighborhood	parents
job	movies	only child	TV

Home and family	School and work	Free time and friends
neighborhood		

B **Answer the questions with your own information. Use short answers.**

1. Are you an only child? *Yes, I am.* **or** *No, I'm not.*
2. Is your neighborhood quiet? _____
3. Do you live with your parents? _____
4. Do you have a big TV? _____
5. Do you and your friends go to college? _____
6. Are you a French major? _____
7. Does your best friend like action movies? _____
8. Is homework fun? _____

2 You and me

Grammar **Complete the conversation with the verb *be*. Use contractions where possible.**

Koji Hi. *I'm* Koji.
Isabel Hi. I _____ Isabel. Where _____ you from, Koji?
Koji I _____ from Japan. How about you?
Isabel Monterrey – in Mexico.
Koji Oh, my friends Manuel and Rosa _____ from Mexico, too.
Isabel Really? _____ they here now?
Koji No, they _____ not. Uh, I guess they _____ late.
Isabel _____ the teacher here?
Koji Yes, she _____. She _____ over there.
Isabel She looks nice. What _____ her name?
Koji I think it _____ Ms. Barnes.

3 I'm Rudy.

Grammar **Answer the questions. Write another piece of information.**

1. Is Rudy from San Francisco?
   No, he's not. He's from Los Angeles.

2. Are his friends English majors?
   _____

3. Do his friends study in the evening?
   _____

4. Does Rudy live alone?
   _____

4 About you 2

Grammar and vocabulary **Unscramble the questions. Then answer the questions with your own information.**

1. name / What's / first / your ? *What's your first name?*
   _____

2. full-time / a / Do / have / you / job ? _____
   _____

3. live / best friend / Does / your / nearby ? _____
   _____

4. weekends / What / do / on / you / do ? _____
   _____

5. does / your neighbor / What / for a living / do ? _____
   _____

6. live / Do / alone / you ? _____
   _____

Lesson B Things in common

1 What doesn't belong?

Vocabulary **Circle the word that doesn't belong in each group.**

1.	apples	(butter)	mangoes	strawberries	4.	baseball	basketball	singing	volleyball
2.	TV	jacket	jeans	sweater	5.	cat	dog	fish	pet
3.	black	color	green	red	6.	dessert	juice	milk	water

2 We're the same.

Grammar **Respond to the statements with *too* or *either*.**

1. I'm a soccer fan.
   I am too.

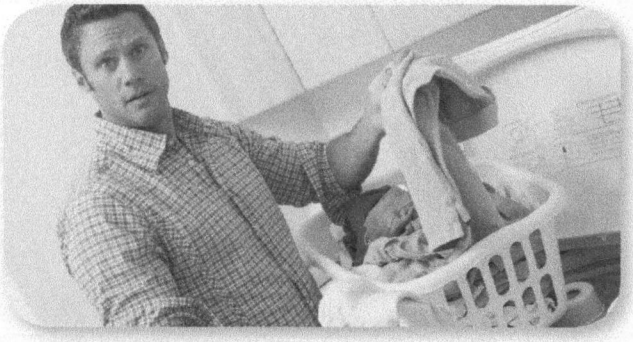

2. I can't stand doing the laundry.
   _____

3. I can sing karaoke all night.
   _____

4. I'm not a good cook.
   _____

5. I don't like shopping.
   _____

6. I love to swim in cold water.
   _____

3 First date

Grammar and vocabulary **Complete the conversations with the expressions in the box. You can use some expressions more than once.**

✓I am too.	I do too.	I can too.
I'm not either.	I don't either.	I can't either.

David You know, I'm always nervous on first dates.
Lesley *I am too.* I guess I'm not very outgoing.
David I guess _____ So, what do you like to do in your free time?
Lesley Well, I go to rock concerts.
David _____ I'm a big fan of Kings of Leon.
Lesley _____ They're my favorite group. I mean, I can listen to their music for hours.
David _____ Do you have all their songs?
Lesley No, I don't. I don't have *The End*.
David _____ But I want to buy it.

Lesley What do you do on the weekends? I mean, do you eat out a lot?
David No. I don't usually go to restaurants.
Lesley _____ I like to eat at home.
David Oh, are you a good cook?
Lesley Um, no. I can't say I'm a good cook.
David _____ But I like to cook.
Lesley Do you ever cook Italian food?
David Sure. I love pasta and pizza.
Lesley _____
David That's amazing! We have a lot in common. Do you like sports? I'm a big sports fan. I watch sports all weekend.
Lesley Oh . . .

4 About you

Grammar and vocabulary **Respond to these statements so they are true for you.**

1. A I always eat chocolate after dinner.
   B *I do too.* **or** *Me too.* **or** *Really? I don't.*
2. A I'm not a baseball fan.
   B _____
3. A I can't drive.
   B _____
4. A I don't have a pet.
   B _____
5. A I'm allergic to bananas.
   B _____
6. A I can cook Italian food.
   B _____

It's cold tonight.

1 Starting a conversation

Conversation strategies

Complete the conversations with the conversation starters in the box.

Is this your first English class here?	You look really nice today. That's a beautiful jacket.
Hi. Are you new here? Do you live around here?	Boy, the food is great. And this cake is really wonderful.
Is it me, or is it kind of noisy in here?	✓Oh, it's cold. Can I close the window?

1. A *Oh, it's cold. Can I close the window?*
   B Sorry, I just opened it. I'm a little warm, actually.

2. A _____
   B Thanks. Actually, it's from China.

3. A _____
   B Thank you. It's my grandmother's recipe.

4. A _____
   B Yes, it is. Are you in this class, too?

5. A _____
   B Yeah, it's pretty loud! Is this your first time here?

6. A _____
   B Uh, no, I don't. I'm actually visiting from Guadalajara.

2 Um, actually, . . .

Conversation strategies **Match each conversation starter with a response.**

1. It's really hot in here. *b*
2. Do you know anyone in this class? ____
3. Do you live in this neighborhood? ____
4. Do you walk to class? ____
5. I like your necklace. ____
6. Do you like coffee? ____

a. Yes, most days. It's actually only five minutes from work.
✓b. It often gets hot in here. But I feel OK today, actually.
c. No, um actually, . . . I'm a little shy.
d. Thanks. It's actually from Colombia.
e. Actually, no, but I work near here.
f. Yeah, I do. Actually, there's a great coffee shop across the street.

3 First day of class

Conversation strategies **Imagine it's the first day of English class. Respond to each conversation starter.**

1. I don't know anyone here. *I don't either, actually. By the way, I'm James.*
2. I feel a little nervous. _____
3. Is it warm in here, or is it me? _____
4. I don't know the teacher's name. _____
5. Are you a friend of Sara's? _____
6. I really like your bag. _____
7. What time does the class finish? _____
8. Do we get a break? _____
9. This is a nice classroom. _____
10. Can we use dictionaries, do you think? _____

Lesson D Making small talk

1 Getting together

Reading **A Read the article. Which of these are good suggestions for making small talk? Check (✓) the boxes.**

- ☐ Don't look at the other person.
- ☐ Keep quiet when the other person is talking.
- ☐ Ask questions that start with *what*, *where*, *how*, or *when*.
- ☐ Have some good topics to discuss.
- ☐ Talk about yourself a lot.

Social Conversations

Eight Tips for Great Social Conversations

Are you shy? Do you find conversations with new people difficult? If you do, then these eight tips can help you connect. If you're outgoing and love to talk, they can help you improve your conversation skills.

1 **Have some topics ready to start a conversation.** Say something about the weather or the place you're in. Talk about the weekend – we all have something to say about weekends!

2 **Make the conversation interesting.** Know about events in the news. Read restaurant and movie reviews. Find out about the current music scene or what's new in fashion or sports.

3 **Be a good listener.** Make eye contact and say, "Yes," "Hmm," "Uh-huh," "Right," and "I know." And say, "Really? That's interesting." It encourages people to talk.

4 **Don't be boring.** Don't just say, "Yes" or "No" when you answer a question. Give some interesting details, too.

5 **Don't talk all the time.** Ask, "How about you?" and show you are interested in the other person, too. People love to talk about themselves!

6 **Ask information questions.** Ask questions like, "What do you do in your free time?" or "What kind of food do you like?" Use follow-up questions to keep the conversation going. But don't ask too many questions – it's not an interview!

7 **Be positive.** Negative comments can sound rude. And if you don't want to answer a personal question, simply say, "Oh, I'm not sure I can answer that," or "I'd rather not say."

8 **Smile!** Everyone loves a smile. Just be relaxed, smile, and be yourself.

B Read the article again and circle the correct words.

1. It's **good** / **not good** to make short responses when you listen.
2. When you answer questions, **you can say** / **don't just reply** "Yes" or "No."
3. Ask **a couple of** / **a lot of** follow-up questions.
4. **Think** / **Don't think** of a conversation like an interview.
5. You **have to** / **don't have to** answer personal questions.

2 Suggestions, please!

Writing **A Rewrite Ben's email to a magazine and the problem page editor's reply. Use correct punctuation.**

New Message

Subject: Suggestions, please

Dear Marcy,
i want to meet new people and make friends the problem is that I'm shy my brother says join a gym or a running club maybe he's right i just hate exercise what can I do?
Ben

Dear Ben,
you need to find people with the same interests what are your hobbies do you read a lot join a book club think about the things you like and find a hobby
Marcy

New Message

Subject: Suggestions, please

Dear Marcy,
I want to meet new people

B Read these questions. Write three suggestions for each question.

1. ***Dave*** I'd like to make friends, but I don't know how. Do you have any suggestions?

_____

_____

2. ***Niki*** I feel shy around new people. How can I improve my conversation skills?

_____

_____

Unit 1 Progress chart

	What can you do? Mark the boxes. ✓ = I can . . . ? = I need to review how to . . .	To review, go back to these pages in the Student's Book.
Grammar	☐ make statements with the simple present and present of *be*. ☐ ask questions with the simple present and present of *be*. ☐ use *too* and *either* to agree.	2, 3, 4, and 5 2 and 3 4 and 5
Vocabulary	☐ use at least 20 words to describe home and family, school and work, and free time and friends.	2 and 3
Conversation strategies	☐ start conversations with people I don't know. ☐ use *actually* to give and "correct" information.	6 and 7 7
Writing	☐ use capital letters, commas, quotation marks, question marks, and periods.	9

Interests

UNIT 2

Lesson A Leisure time

1 What do they like to do?

Grammar **Complete the sentences. Use the correct form of the verbs in the box. Sometimes there is more than one correct answer.**

cook dance draw play ✓read work out

1. Pam and Victor aren't interested in *reading* books. They both prefer *to read* magazines. They really enjoy *reading* fashion magazines.

2. Ian would like _____ every day. He doesn't like _____ in the gym. He enjoys _____ at home.

3. Sun Hee can't _____. She's interested in _____ and would like _____ the tango.

4. Tom isn't good at _____ people. He hates _____ people, but he can _____ animals very well.

5. Amy and Dave usually like _____, but they can't _____ Italian food. They prefer _____ Chinese food.

6. Erica can't _____ the guitar very well. She enjoys _____ music, but she's not very good at _____ it.

2 At home

Grammar **Complete the sentences. Use the correct form of the verbs in the box. Sometimes there is more than one correct answer.**

bowl	go	ski	try
✓exercise	play	swim	watch

Linda You and I watch too much TV. We need some exercise.
James I know, but I don't really enjoy *exercising*.
Linda But you like _____ tennis, right?
James Yeah, but these days I prefer _____ tennis on TV.
Linda How about bowling? You're good at _____.
James Yeah, but it's always noisy at the bowling alley.
Linda I guess you're right.
James Well, we can both _____. And the pool's nearby.
Linda But it's always crowded.
James Oh, I know! We both like _____.
Linda Actually, I can't stand the cold and snow.
James Really? Well, are you interested in _____ something new?
Linda Sure. I'd like _____ to the new Thai restaurant in our neighborhood.
James Great idea, Linda. Let's think about exercising tomorrow.

3 About you

Grammar and vocabulary **Answer the questions with true information. Add more information.**

1. A What are you good at?
   B *Well, I'm pretty good at learning languages. I can speak Portuguese and French.*

2. A What are you bad at?
   B _____

3. A Would you like to play a musical instrument?
   B _____

4. A What movie do you want to see?
   B _____

5. A What do you really hate doing?
   B _____

6. A What do you enjoy doing on the weekends?
   B _____

1 All kinds of music

Vocabulary **Look at the pictures. Write the type of music.**

1. *folk music*

2. j

3. r

4. l

5. c

6. c

7. p

8. r

2 What's new?

Grammar **Complete Kevin's email with the correct words.**

New Message

To: Sam_P@cup.com
From: KevinJ@cup.com
Subject: My new job

Hi Sam,

Guess what! I have a new job at a café. They play some great music here so it's a great job for ___*me*___ (me / it). I really like _____ (him / it).

They play music by some great bands, like Maroon 5. Do you know _____ (her / them)? Then there's Bruno Mars. He's cool. I really like _____ (him / it), too. Actually, I think almost everybody in the café _____ (is / are) a Bruno Mars fan. Do you like country music? I don't really care for _____ (it / him). No one I know really _____ (like / likes) country. But I think Taylor Swift is cool, and she has a great new album. Do you know _____ (us / her)?

Oh, did I tell you? I'm in a band with some friends at the café. They're really great. I want you to meet _____ (him / them). We play hip-hop. But no one in my family _____ (come / comes) to listen to _____ (him / us). They don't like hip-hop! But that's OK.

What's new with you? Write soon.

Kevin

3 Talking about music

Grammar **Complete the questions with object pronouns. Then answer the questions.**

1. A Beyoncé's a great singer. She's pretty, too.
   Do you like *her* ?
   B *Yes, I do. She's amazing.*
2. A You know Justin Timberlake, right? I think he's great.
   What do you think of _____ ?
   B _____
3. A You know, I'm not a fan of jazz. How about you?
   Do you ever listen to _____ ?
   B _____
4. A Hey, the Black Keys were on TV last night. They're a really cool band. Do you know _____ ?
   B _____
5. A My mom and dad love Sarah Chang. She's their favorite violinist. Do your parents like _____ ?
   B _____
6. A Do you like Latin music? Jeff and I have tickets for the Shakira concert. Do you want to go with _____ ?
   B _____
7. A I don't usually like country bands, but I love Lady Antebellum. Do you know _____ ?
   B _____

4 About you

Grammar and vocabulary **Answer the questions using object pronouns. Then give more information.**

1. Do you like Alicia Keys? *Yes, I like her a lot. She has some great songs.* **or** *Actually, I don't know her.*
2. What do you think of the Rolling Stones? _____
3. Do you like Mariah Carey? _____
4. Do you listen to pop music very often? _____
5. What do you think of folk music? _____
6. Do you and your friends ever go to concerts? _____
7. What do you think of Bruno Mars? _____
8. Do you know the band The Lumineers? _____

Lesson C I'm not really into it.

1 Saying *no*

Conversation strategies **Complete the conversations with the sentences in the box.**

Not really. He just watches TV a lot.	✓ Not really. My mom knitted it for me last year.
Actually, no. My sister got it at the bakery.	No, but he collects caps.
Well, no. I like to make peanut butter cookies.	No. I'm not really good with my hands.
Um, no. He just uses it for computer games.	Not really. Well, I guess his computer is a hobby.

1. Jenny I really like your sweater. Is it new?
   Keiko *Not really. My mom knitted it for me last year.*
   Jenny It's really nice. So, can you knit, too?
   Keiko _____ But I bake a little.
   Jenny Oh, did you make this cake?
   Keiko _____
   But I like to make cookies sometimes.
   Jenny Me too. Do you ever make chocolate chip cookies?
   Keiko _____
   My new boyfriend loves them!

2. Mike I want to buy a Yankees baseball cap for my brother.
   Greg Why? Is it his birthday?
   Mike _____
   Does your brother collect anything?
   Greg My brother? _____
   Mike But he can't watch it all the time. Does he have any hobbies?
   Greg _____
   Mike Oh, yeah? My brother is on the computer all the time.
   Greg Oh, does he use it for homework?
   Mike _____

2 No, not really.

Conversation strategies **Complete the responses to make them more friendly.**

1. A Do you go online a lot?
   B Not really. *I don't have a computer.*
2. A What a great photo! Are you interested in photography?
   B No. _____
3. A I really enjoy my piano lessons. Would you like to learn to play the piano?
   B Um, no. _____
4. A I love growing flowers and vegetables. Do you enjoy gardening?
   B Well, not really. _____

3 Yes and no

Conversation strategies **Answer the questions in a friendly way. Use *really* in each answer.**

1. A Are you good at fixing things?
   B No, *not really. I'm not good with my hands*.
   C Yes, *I'm really good at fixing cars*.

2. A Do you make your own clothes?
   B No, _____.
   C Yes, _____.

3. A Does your best friend collect anything?
   B No, _____.
   C Yes, _____.

4. A Does your teacher speak Russian?
   B No, _____.
   C Yes, _____.

5. A Are you into winter sports, like skiing?
   B No, _____.
   C Yes, _____.

6. A Do you and your friends enjoy cooking?
   B Um, no, _____.
   C Yes, _____.

7. A Are your classmates into computer games?
   B No, _____.
   C Yes, _____.

8. A Are you interested in photography?
   B No, _____.
   C Yes, _____.

4 About you

Conversation strategies **Answer the questions with your own information. Use *really* in your answers.**

1. Are you into sports?
   Yes, I really like soccer and volleyball. **or** *No, not really. I prefer doing artistic things.*

2. Would you like to learn a new language?
   _____

3. Do you have a lot of hobbies?
   _____

4. Can you knit or sew?
   _____

5. Are you artistic?
   _____

Lesson D Online forums

1 Popular interests

Reading **A Read the online forum posts. Write the correct topic for each post.**

✓Cooking	Music	Photography	Running	Water sports
Fashion	Pets	Reading	Technology	Winter sports

Denver Hobby Forum

▶ *Cooking*

From: sushifreak
I want to learn how to make Japanese food, especially sushi. Do you have any easy recipe ideas?

▶ _____

From: ladiva
I enjoy singing, and I want to start a jazz band. I'm looking for piano and trumpet players. Please email me at ladiva@cup.org.

▶ _____

From: trailblazer
I just started running. I really want to run a marathon. Can anyone suggest good places to train in the city?

▶ _____

From: sunriser
I love to take pictures, especially sunrises. Does anyone know a good place to take pictures? I'd prefer a place that's close to my house, if possible.

▶ _____

From: grungeking
I want to find a good place for vintage clothes in Portland, Maine. I also want to buy shoes and accessories. Any ideas?

▶ _____

From: teacher
I love using apps for just about everything. I want to create my own app to help people learn Spanish. Can anyone recommend a good company for building apps?

▶ _____

From: snowthrills
I'm good at skiing, and I'd like to try snowboarding. Can anyone suggest a good teacher?

▶ _____

From: heartbroken
We have a beautiful gray cat – free to a good home in the New York area. We can't keep her because I just found out I'm allergic to cats.

B Read the responses to the posts below. Who are they for? Match the responses with the writers of the posts. Write *a* to *h*.

1. I like to run the track at Livingston Park. __c__
2. IceCat Technology makes good software. ____
3. I'm pretty good at playing the piano. Let's jam! ____
4. We'd love to have her! We live in Bergen County. ____
5. I take pictures at Keystone Park. It has great views. ____
6. Try www.50s.cup.com. They have great 1950s dresses and stuff. ____
7. I can send you my recipe for *kayu*. It's delicious! ____
8. Call the ski resort and ask for an experienced instructor. ____

a. teacher
b. heartbroken
✓c. trailblazer
d. snowthrills
e. sushifreak
f. ladiva
g. sunriser
h. grungeking

2 My favorite hobby

Writing **A Complete the post with *and, but, or, also, because,* or *especially*. Sometimes there is more than one correct answer.**

Message Board

Rock climbing

One of my hobbies is rock climbing. I go once or twice a month with my family ___or___ friends. We like to climb the mountains near my house _____ they're really beautiful _____ the views are wonderful. We often go to Bear Mountain _____ Kennedy Park. I prefer Kennedy Park _____ it's closer. Kennedy Park _____ has a great campground.

It's great to be outdoors, _____ the weather isn't always very good. When it's raining _____ snowing, climbing can be very dangerous _____ the rocks get wet and slippery.

In the winter, my friends _____ I sometimes go rock climbing indoors, usually on a Saturday _____ Sunday. There's a climbing wall at the mall, _____ it's not the same. We prefer to be outdoors, _____ in the summer.

B Write about one of your hobbies.

One of my hobbies is

Unit 2 Progress chart

	What can you do? Mark the boxes. ✓ = I can . . . ? = I need to review how to . . .	To review, go back to these pages in the Student's Book.
Grammar	☐ make statements with different verb forms.	12 and 13
	☐ ask questions with different verb forms.	12 and 13
	☐ use the correct verb forms after other verbs, modal verbs, and prepositions.	12 and 13
	☐ use object pronouns, and the pronouns *everybody* and *nobody*.	15
Vocabulary	☐ name at least 8 common interests.	12 and 13
	☐ name at least 8 hobbies.	12, 13, 16, and 17
	☐ name at least 8 kinds of music.	14 and 15
Conversation strategies	☐ say *no* in a polite and friendly way.	16 and 17
	☐ use *really* and *not really* to make statements stronger or softer.	17
Writing	☐ use *and, but, or, also, especially,* or *because* to link ideas.	19

Health

UNIT 3

Lesson A Healthy living

1 Staying in shape

Grammar **Complete the conversations with the correct form of the verbs.**

1. Max Hi, Carl. How ___is___ it ___going___ (go)?
   Carl Great. What _____ you _____ (do)?
   Max Oh. I _____ (try) to get in shape before graduation.
   Carl So _____ you _____ (try) to lose weight?
   Max Yeah, a little. I _____ (want) to look good in the photo. So this month I _____ (exercise) and _____ (eat) salads. And I _____ (cut) down on fried food and things like that.
   Carl Good for you. You know, I _____ (read) an interesting book about healthy eating right now. _____ you _____ (want) to borrow it?
   Max Sure. Thanks. But you always _____ (look) so good. You _____ (not need) to lose weight.
   Carl Well, it's probably because I usually _____ (eat) healthy foods and I _____ (exercise) most days.

2. Doctor So, Paul, you _____ (want) to improve your lifestyle.
   Paul Yes, I _____ (need) to get into shape. I know I _____ (not get) enough exercise right now, but I _____ (not have) the energy.
   Doctor So, what exercise _____ you _____ (do) these days?
   Paul Actually, I _____ (not get) any exercise at all. I _____ (work) on a big project for my job, and I _____ (not have) a lot of time. Life's kind of stressful right now.
   Doctor So how _____ you usually _____ (cope) with stress?
   Paul Well, right now, I _____ (not cope) really. Usually I _____ (not eat) a lot of snacks and chocolate, but I _____ (eat) a lot of them now.
   Doctor So _____ you usually _____ (have) a healthy diet?
   Paul Well, it's not bad, I guess. I _____ (love) red meat, and I _____ (eat) that every day. I _____ really _____ (not like) vegetables, so I _____ often _____ (not eat) them.
   Doctor Well, I think you _____ (need) to eat a balanced diet and to get more exercise. Try this plan for four weeks. Then come back in two weeks so we can review it.
   Paul OK. Thanks.

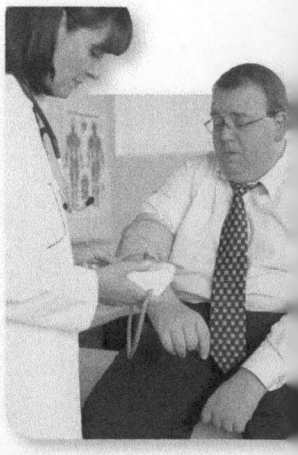

2 Susan's lifestyle

Grammar **Look at the picture and complete the email with the correct form of the verbs in the box.**

do drink drink eat have not buy not do not try play want ✓work out

New Message

To: Cassie_90_P@cup.com
From: Marcy@cup.com
Subject: My new roommate

Hey Cassie. Do you want to meet my new roommate? You'd like her. She is SO healthy. I'm writing emails, and she *'s working out* on her new exercise bike. She _____ to lose weight or anything, but she says that she _____ to stay healthy. And look – she _____ water, too! I mean, I _____ soda – but not her! She _____ a pretty healthy diet and lifestyle. She _____ a lot of fruit, and she _____ much junk food. Usually, she _____ tennis once a month, but now she _____ karate twice a week, too. I really need to do something like that. I _____ anything to stay healthy. :)

3 About you

Grammar and vocabulary **Are these sentences true or false for you? Write *T* (true) or *F* (false). Then correct the false statements.**

1. *F* I'm drinking a lot of milk these days.
   I'm not drinking a lot of milk these days. I'm drinking a lot of soda.
2. ____ My best friend eats junk food every day.
   _____
3. ____ I'm not taking any classes right now.
   _____
4. ____ I sleep for five hours a night.
   _____
5. ____ My friends have a lot of stress in their lives.
   _____
6. ____ My family doesn't get any exercise at all.
   _____

Aches and pains

1 What's the matter?

Vocabulary **A** There are seven health problems in the puzzle. Find the other six. Look in these directions (→ ↓).

A	T	O	O	T	H	A	C	H	E	W	A
B	C	K	F	M	U	U	O	E	R	F	L
S	O	R	E	T	H	R	O	A	T	D	L
R	U	I	V	D	E	I	H	D	U	J	E
V	G	J	P	L	A	R	U	P	L	A	F
E	H	C	S	H	E	A	D	A	C	H	E
S	I	O	T	B	J	W	L	S	A	N	V
O	H	L	F	O	V	A	O	U	B	D	E
B	E	A	L	L	E	R	G	I	E	S	R
G	A	N	G	D	C	K	S	W	N	C	H
S	T	O	M	A	C	H	A	C	H	E	I
R	M	R	L	T	N	F	R	G	C	S	R

B Look at the picture. Write sentences with the words from part A.

1. *Joe has a fever.*
2. _____
3. _____
4. _____
5. _____
6. _____
7. _____

2 I feel sick.

Grammar and vocabulary **Look at the pictures. Write questions and answers.**

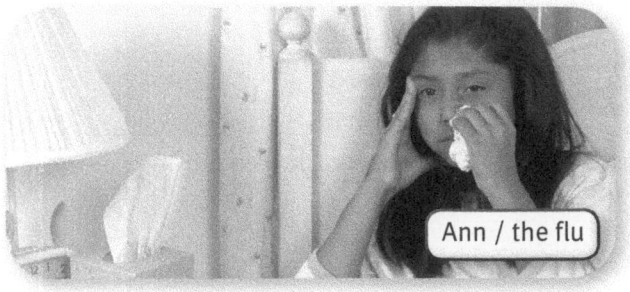

1. *What does Ann do when she has the flu?*
   When *Ann has the flu, she stays in bed* .

2. _____
   If _____ .

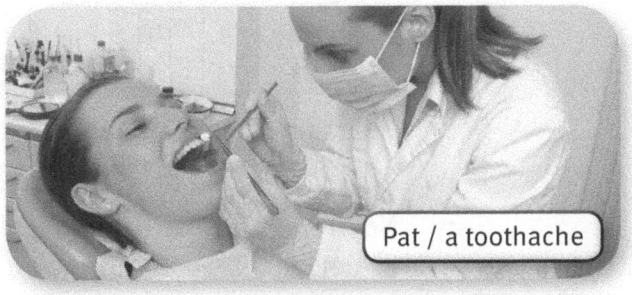

3. _____
   _____ when _____ .

4. _____
   _____ if _____ .

3 About you

Grammar and vocabulary **Write questions for a friend using *when* or *if*. Then answer your friend's questions.**

1. You *What do you do when you're sick?*
   (when / are sick)
   Friend When I'm sick, I stay home and watch movies all day. How about you?
   You _____

2. You _____
   (if / have a bad cough)
   Friend I usually take cough medicine if I have a bad cough. What do you do?
   You _____

3. You _____
   (if / get an upset stomach)
   Friend If I get an upset stomach, I drink water. I don't eat a lot. How about you?
   You _____

4. You _____
   (when / have a fever)
   Friend When I have a fever, I take aspirin and I don't go out. What about you?
   You _____

Lesson C Really? How come?

1 It's my allergies.

Conversation strategies **Complete the conversation. Use the sentences in the box.**

Are you serious? How come? I mean, why not?
✓ Oh, no! That's too bad. Do you sneeze a lot?
You're kidding! So you never take medicine?
Headaches? Do you take anything?
Gosh, that's terrible! So, what are you studying?
Really? So how do you study when you don't feel good?

Joan Gary, are you OK? Your eyes are all red.

Gary Oh, it's my allergies. I always feel this way in the spring.

Joan *Oh, no! That's too bad. Do you sneeze a lot?*

Gary Yeah. I sneeze all the time. And I get headaches, too.

Joan _____

Gary Not really. Actually, I don't like to take medicine.

Joan _____

Gary No. Never. And especially allergy medicine. If I take it, I can't study.

Joan _____

Gary Well, you see, when I take medicine, I always fall asleep.

Joan _____

Gary It's hard, but I have to try. Right now I'm studying for a big test next week.

Joan _____

Gary I'm studying medicine!

2 You're kidding!

Conversation strategies **Circle the best response to show surprise.**

1. My husband talks in his sleep.
   a. My husband does, too.
   (b) Wow! What does he say?

2. I love getting up early on weekends.
   a. Do you get up early on weekdays, too?
   b. Are you serious? On weekends?

3. I take two or three naps every day.
   a. Gosh! Do you sleep OK at night?
   b. I know. I saw you fall asleep in class once!

4. I often drink hot chocolate if I can't sleep.
   a. Me too. I love hot chocolate at night.
   b. You're kidding! It keeps me awake.

5. My grandmother goes running six days a week.
   a. No way! How old is she?
   b. So she's really into exercise, huh?

6. I often dream about food.
   a. I do too. I always dream about ice cream.
   b. Really? Are you hungry when you go to bed?

7. I have three part-time jobs.
   a. Oh, wow! You work really hard.
   b. Do you often get tired?

8. If I can't sleep, I often listen to rock music.
   a. Gosh! I can't sleep with music on.
   b. Me too. I also listen to pop music.

3 No way!

Conversation strategies **Write responses to show surprise. Then ask follow-up questions.**

1. A One of my friends cleans the house when he can't sleep.
   B *No way!* *So does he go back to bed at all?*
2. A My best friend remembers all her dreams.
   B _____ _____
3. A I sometimes sleep at the office.
   B _____ _____
4. A Sometimes I can't sleep because my neighbors play loud music.
   B _____ _____
5. A My little brother has the same nightmare about once a month.
   B _____ _____
6. A My father sleepwalks every night.
   B _____ _____
7. A I never use an alarm clock.
   B _____ _____
8. A My sister goes running right after she eats dinner.
   B _____ _____

4 About you

Conversation strategies **Answer the questions with your own information.**

1. Are you feeling sleepy right now? _____
2. How often do you take naps on weekdays? _____
3. Do you ever sleep in class or at work? _____
4. Are you sleeping well these days? _____
5. What do you do when you wake up at night? _____
6. Do you dream in color? _____

1 Understanding stress

Reading **A Read the leaflet. Which of these are signs of stress? Check (✓) the boxes.**

- ☐ You have health problems.
- ☐ You can't concentrate.
- ☐ You have a lot of energy.
- ☐ You are tired.
- ☐ You breathe slowly.
- ☐ You feel irritable.

Common Questions About Stress

Am I stressed?

If you can't sleep well or can't concentrate, . . .
If you feel depressed or want to cry a lot, . . .
If you have a headache or an upset stomach, . . .
If you can't relax and you feel irritable, . . .
If you are extremely tired, . . .

. . . then it's possible you are stressed.

Is stress bad for me?

Occasional stress is common and not always bad for you. However, if you feel stressed for a long time, it can be serious. Stress can make you sick. It can also affect your memory or concentration, so it's hard to get your work done.

What can I do?

Fortunately, there's a lot you can do. Try some of these relaxation techniques. If you still feel stressed, then make an appointment to see your doctor.

Relaxation Techniques

1. **Breathe** Take a breath, hold it for four seconds, and then breathe out very slowly. Feel your body relax.
2. **Exercise** Walk or exercise for just 30 minutes each day and feel better.

3. **Talk** Call a friend. Talk about your problems.
4. **Meditate** Close your eyes and focus on something calm. Feel relaxed.
5. **Pamper yourself** Take a hot bath, or have a massage.

6. **Do something you enjoy** Listen to music. Sing. Watch TV. Meet a friend for coffee.

Department of Health – "Take care of yourself."

B Read the leaflet again. Then choose the correct words to complete the sentences.

1. When you're stressed, it's not easy to ___*relax*___.	a. relax	b. cry
2. Stress _____ a lot of people.	a. affects	b. doesn't affect
3. Stress is _____ good for you.	a. sometimes	b. never
4. If you're very stressed, you often can't _____.	a. exercise	b. think
5. One good relaxation technique is to _____.	a. see a doctor	b. take a bath

2 Healthy lifestyles

Writing **A** **Read these suggestions for a healthy lifestyle. Add commas where necessary.**

Healthy Habits

BY DR. GOODMAN

Take yoga classes. When you practice yoga, you stay in shape and relax at the same time.

If you can't sleep drink a glass of warm milk.

Sing at home or in your car if you want to have a lot of energy.

When you listen to music choose relaxing music.

If you feel sad take a long walk. Exercise can help your mood.

Do something you love when life is stressful.

B **Choose one of the titles below and write a short article. Give three suggestions.**

Sleep **Food and Diet** **Exercise**

Unit 3 Progress chart

	What can you do? Mark the boxes. ✓ = I can . . . ? = I need to review how to . . .	To review, go back to these pages in the Student's Book.
Grammar	☐ make statements with the simple present and present continuous.	22 and 23
	☐ ask questions with the simple present and present continuous.	22 and 23
	☐ use *if* and *when* in statements and questions.	25
Vocabulary	☐ name at least 8 healthy habits.	22 and 23
	☐ name at least 4 unhealthy habits.	22 and 23
	☐ name at least 6 health problems.	24 and 25
Conversation strategies	☐ keep a conversation going with comments and follow-up questions.	26 and 27
	☐ use expressions like *Wow!* or *You're kidding!* to show surprise.	27
Writing	☐ use commas in *if* and *when* clauses.	29

Celebrations

UNIT 4

Lesson A Birthdays

1 What month is it?

Vocabulary **A** **Write the months in the correct order.**

1. *January* 4. _____ 7. _____ 10. _____
2. _____ 5. _____ 8. _____ 11. _____
3. _____ 6. _____ 9. _____ 12. _____

B **Complete the sentences with the correct numbers.**

1. January is the *first* month of the year.
2. March is the _____ month of the year.
3. June is the _____ month of the year.
4. July is the _____ month of the year.
5. October is the _____ month of the year.
6. December is the _____ month of the year.

2 When's her birthday?

Grammar and vocabulary **Look at the dates. Then write each person's birthday two ways.**

1. *Halle Berry's birthday is on August fourteenth.*
   Her birthday is on the fourteenth of August.
2. _____
   _____
3. _____
   _____
4. _____
   _____
5. _____
   _____
6. _____
   _____

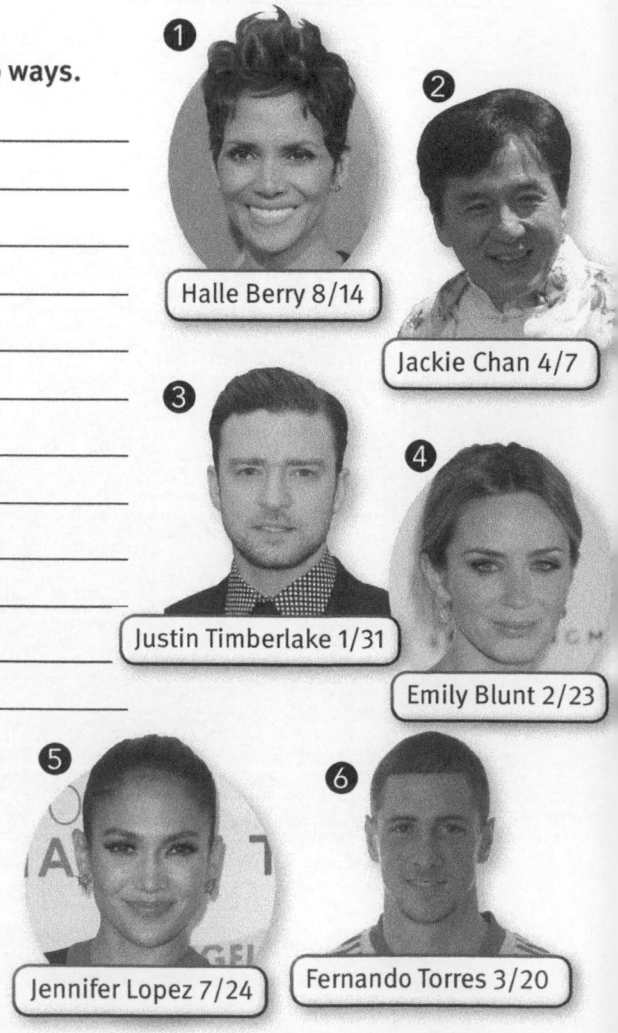

3 Future plans

Grammar **Complete the conversations with the correct form of *be going to*.**

1. Sam What *are you going to do* (you / do) this weekend?
   Diane I _____ (see) my grandmother. We _____ (have) a birthday party for her.
   Sam That's nice. How _____ (you / celebrate)? I mean, _____ (it / be) a big party?
   Diane No, not really. We _____ (not do) much. It _____ (be) just the family. Mom _____ (bake) her a cake. Then her friends _____ (take) her dancing. She's a tango teacher.
   Sam Your grandmother's a tango teacher? Cool.

2. Yumi That was Jun on the phone. He can't take us to Sarah's party.
   Kara Oh, no. Why not?
   Yumi No car. His parents _____ (go) away this weekend, and they _____ (take) the car.
   Kara Huh. Where _____ (they / go)? Well, anyway, _____ Dan _____ (be) there?
   Yumi Yeah, but he _____ (not go) until after work.
   Kara Well, it looks like we _____ (have to) walk. Wear comfortable shoes!

4 Happy birthday!

Grammar and vocabulary **Complete the card. Put the words in order.**

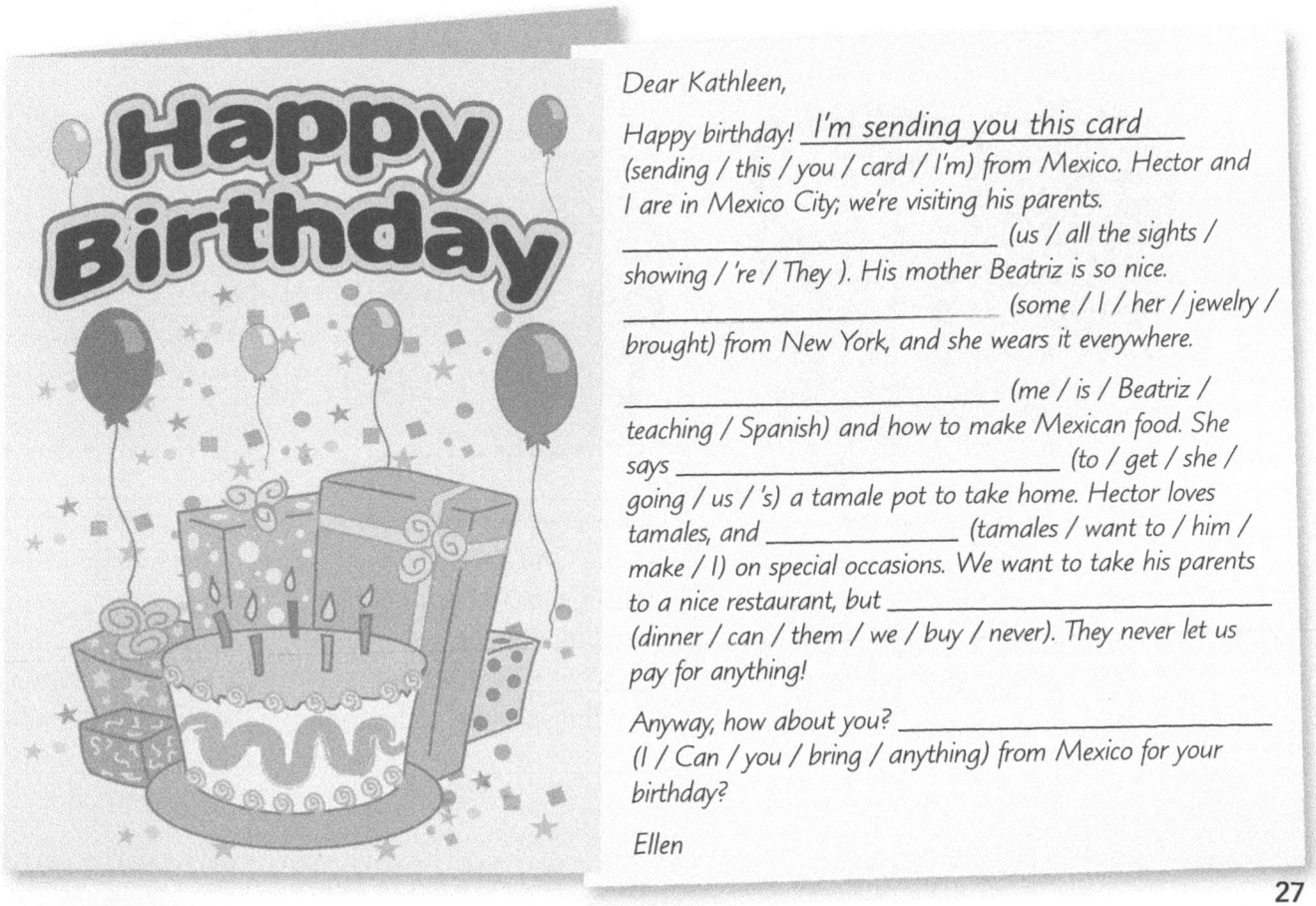

Dear Kathleen,

Happy birthday! *I'm sending you this card* *(sending / this / you / card / I'm) from Mexico. Hector and I are in Mexico City; we're visiting his parents.*
_____ *(us / all the sights / showing / 're / They). His mother Beatriz is so nice.*
_____ *(some / I / her / jewelry / brought) from New York, and she wears it everywhere.*

_____ *(me / is / Beatriz / teaching / Spanish) and how to make Mexican food. She says* _____ *(to / get / she / going / us / 's) a tamale pot to take home. Hector loves tamales, and* _____ *(tamales / want to / him / make / I) on special occasions. We want to take his parents to a nice restaurant, but* _____ *(dinner / can / them / we / buy / never). They never let us pay for anything!*

Anyway, how about you? _____ *(I / Can / you / bring / anything) from Mexico for your birthday?*

Ellen

1 Good times

Vocabulary **Look at the pictures. Write the special event. Then complete the descriptions with the expressions in the box.**

blow out (the) candle	go out for a romantic dinner	shout "Happy New Year"
exchange rings	go trick-or-treating	sing "Happy Birthday"
get a diploma	have a reception	✓ wear a cap and gown
give her chocolates	see the fireworks	wear costumes

1. Ana and her classmates have to *wear a cap and gown*. When they call her name, Ana's going to _____.

2. The waiters _____ when they bring out a cake. Erin's going to make a wish and _____.

3. Allen and Carine decided to _____. After dinner, Allen's going to _____.

4. Bruce and Sheila are at a big party on the beach. They wanted to _____. At midnight, they're going to _____.

5. Ahmad and Keisha are getting married. During the wedding, they're going to _____. After the wedding, they're going to _____.

6. John and Blake love to _____ of their favorite comic-book characters. When they're ready, they're going to _____ in the neighborhood.

2 A busy week

Grammar **Read George's calendar. Write a sentence about each plan. Use the present continuous.**

MAY						
Sunday	Monday	Tuesday	Wednesday	Thursday	Friday	Saturday
8 Mother's Day – have lunch with Mom	9 **8:00** – Meet Ann for dinner	10 Play tennis with Greg after work	11 **8:00** – See a movie with Joe	12 Work out with Dan before work	13 **2:00** – Give a speech at Keith and Karen's wedding	14 **5:00** – Go to Jennifer's graduation party

1. *On May eighth, George is having lunch with his mother.*
2. _____
3. _____
4. _____
5. _____
6. _____
7. _____

3 What's going to happen?

Grammar **Write a prediction about each picture. Use *be going to*. Some are negative.**

1. *It's going to rain.*
(rain)

2. _____
(go trick-or-treating)

3. _____
(give / flowers)

4. _____
(see / fireworks)

5. _____
(get a diploma)

6. _____
(be sunny)

Lesson C It depends.

1 "Vague" expressions

Conversation strategies **Rewrite the underlined words, if possible, using vague expressions like *and everything, and stuff (like that)*, or *and things (like that)*. You can't rewrite some of them.**

1. Maya Let's do something different this year for New Year's. Like take a vacation.

Jake OK. We work hard, and I think we really need a break.

Maya Yes, I'd like to go away on vacation and lie on a beach and read ~~and relax and sleep~~ *and stuff*.

Jake Yeah, and then in the evenings we can have some nice romantic dinners with candles and music and nice food.

Maya Or we can go to movies and concerts and listen to local bands and singers.

Jake Could you give me my tablet? We can look online, and I'm sure we can find a nice place to go.

Maya Just one thing. Who's going to tell everyone, especially your parents, that we're not going to be at the family party this year?

2. Sonia Hey, there's a Rodeo Days festival today and tomorrow. What is it exactly?

Pete Well, every February they have this festival, and all the kids dress up in cowboy costumes with cowboy boots and hats and scarves. And they ride horses, and there's a parade and competitions and exhibits. So what do you think? Do you want to go?

Sonia Maybe. I don't know, I'm not big on rodeos and cowboys and horses.

Pete Well, it's really kind of fun. And people sell jewelry and T-shirts and belts and boots and hats.

Sonia Well, that sounds fun.

Pete And they have cowboy food like beans and steak and other kinds of cowboy food.

Sonia Oh, OK. So let's go – maybe this afternoon?

2 About you

Conversation strategies **Answer the questions with the responses in the box. Use each response only once. Then add more information.**

✓I don't know. I'm not sure. It depends. Maybe.

1. Are you going to celebrate your birthday with a party and everything?
   I don't know. My girlfriend usually surprises me on my birthday.
2. What do you want to do this weekend?
   _____
3. Are you going to send your mother some flowers on her birthday?
   _____
4. Do you want to go see the fireworks tonight?
   _____

3 Scrambled conversation

Conversation strategies **Number the lines of the conversation in the correct order.**

- [ ] But you can also shop for cool Chinese gifts and things.
- [1] Would you like to go to a Chinese festival?
- [ ] Well, maybe. What do people do?
- [ ] There's going to be free food? Great, I'd love to go.
- [ ] Well, I don't know. I'm not big on dances and stuff like that.
- [ ] Well, at least the food is great, and it's free.
- [ ] Uh, maybe, but I don't have money for shopping right now.
- [ ] It's for Chinese New Year.
- [ ] Lots of things, like lion dances, fireworks, and everything!
- [ ] I'm not sure. What kind of festival is it exactly?

1 Celebrating mothers

Reading **A Read the article. Then add the correct heading to each paragraph.**

History of the holiday
Ideas for Mother's Day
Traditional ways to celebrate
When is Mother's Day?
✓Why people celebrate Mother's Day

Mother's Day

Why people celebrate Mother's Day

In many countries, there is a special day of the year when children of all ages celebrate their mothers. On this day – Mother's Day – children tell their mothers that they love them, and thank them for their love and care.

_____

Mother's Day is not a new celebration. Historians say that it started as a spring festival in ancient Greece. The modern festival of Mother's Day probably comes from England in the 1600s, when people had a day off from their jobs to visit their mothers on a day they called "Mothering Sunday." They took small gifts and a special cake called "simnel cake." In the United States, Mother's Day became an official holiday in 1914.

_____

People in different countries celebrate Mother's Day on different days. In Spain and Portugal, Mother's Day is the first Sunday in May. In Australia, Brazil, Italy, Japan, Turkey, and the United States, it's on the second Sunday in May, whereas in France and Sweden, it's on the last Sunday in May. In Argentina, Mother's Day is celebrated on the third Sunday in October.

_____

Although many countries celebrate Mother's Day at different times of the year, the holidays have one purpose in common – to show love and appreciation for mothers. For example, on Mother's Day morning, some children give their mothers gifts they made especially for this holiday.

_____

What are you going to do next Mother's Day? Maybe you can use some of these ideas to make your mother feel special.

- *Make or buy your mother a beautiful Mother's Day card*
- *Write her a letter telling her why you appreciate her*
- *Make her a special meal or bake a cake*
- *Plant a flower or tree somewhere she can see it*

B Read the article again. Answer the questions.

1. Where did the idea of Mother's Day come from originally? *It came from ancient Greece.*
2. Which country started the tradition of giving presents on Mother's Day? _____
3. What was Mother's Day called in England? _____
4. When do Brazil and Japan celebrate Mother's Day? _____
5. What do you do on Mother's Day? _____

2 Making plans

Writing **A** **Start and end these notes to different people.**

An email to a friend

New Message
To: steve_P@cup.com
Subject: MY PARTY

Hi Steve,

I'm having a party on Saturday night. Everybody's going to be there. Hope you can make it.

See you then.

A note to your neighbor

_____

I'm having a party on Friday. We're going to have a band. I hope it's not too noisy. Please join us.

_____

An email to your teacher

New Message
To: MsSmith@cup.com
Subject: Class

_____

I can't come to class tomorrow. I have a fever and a headache, so I'm going to see the doctor.

_____

B **Write to these people about a special celebration.**

An email to a teacher

New Message
To:
Subject:

A note to a friend

An email to your grandparents

New Message
To:
Subject:

Unit 4 Progress chart

	What can you do? Mark the boxes. ✓ = I can . . . ? = I need to review how to . . .	To review, go back to these pages in the Student's Book.
Grammar	☐ use *be going to* for the future.	35, 36, and 37
	☐ use indirect objects and indirect object pronouns.	34 and 35
	☐ use the present continuous for specific future plans.	37
Vocabulary	☐ say dates with the months of the year and ordinal numbers.	34
	☐ describe things people do on holidays and special days.	34
Conversation strategies	☐ use "vague" expressions like *and everything* and *and things*.	38 and 39
	☐ use "vague" responses like *I don't know* and *Maybe*.	39
Writing	☐ start and end invitations, emails, and personal notes.	41

Growing up

UNIT 5

Lesson A Childhood

1 What's the year?

Vocabulary **Write the years in numbers or words.**

1. twenty ten *2010*
2. nineteen oh-four _____
3. two thousand eight _____
4. nineteen seventy-seven _____
5. 1982 *nineteen eighty-two*
6. 2006 _____
7. 2013 _____
8. 1998 _____

2 Talking about the past

Grammar **Complete the conversations with *was*, *wasn't*, *were*, *weren't*, *did*, or *didn't*.**

1. **Rick** So, Dina, *did* you grow up here in Miami?
   Dina Yes, I _____, but we _____ born here. My sister and I _____ born in Puerto Rico, and we moved here when we _____ kids.
   Rick So, _____ you study English when you _____ in school in Puerto Rico?
   Dina Yes, we _____ – for a few years – but we _____ really learn English until we came here.
   Rick Wow! And now you speak English better than I do – and I _____ born here!

2. **Thomas** When *were* you born, Grandma?
   Grandma I _____ born in 1934.
   Thomas Really? _____ you born here in Los Angeles?
   Grandma No, I _____. Your grandfather and I _____ both born in China.
   Thomas So when _____ you come to the U.S.?
   Grandma My family _____ move here until I _____ 13 years old.
   Thomas Really? So _____ you sad to leave all your friends and family in China?
   Grandma Yes, we _____. But we _____ sad for long. We soon made friends and everything.
   Thomas That's good. When _____ Grandpa born?
   Grandma He _____ born in 1933, but he says he _____ really born until 1952.
   Thomas Why does he say that?
   Grandma Because that's when he met *me*!

3 A life story

Grammar **Complete the story with the words in the box. You can use some words more than once.**

✓ago for from in last long then to until when

This is a picture of my best friend, Mi-young. I took it a few years *ago* . Mi-young and I met _____ 1994. We were very young _____ we became friends. Mi-young is a very interesting person. She was born in Busan, South Korea, _____ 1990. Her family moved to the U.S. _____ she was three years old. They lived in Chicago _____ Mi-young was 15. _____ they moved to New York City. I cried _____ a long time after they moved.

Mi-young didn't live in New York _____ because she came back to Chicago for college _____ she was 18. We were roommates at the University of Chicago _____ four years – _____ 2008 _____ 2012. We graduated and shared an apartment _____ a few months. _____ she got a great job in Phoenix, Arizona, and moved there. I really missed her, but guess what? _____ month she called and said there's a perfect job for me at her company. So I'm going there _____ October for an interview, and I can't wait!

4 About you

Grammar and vocabulary **Write questions using the prompts given. Then answer the questions with your own information.**

1. When / you born ? *When were you born?* _____
_____
2. Where / your parents born ? _____
_____
3. Where / you grow up ? _____
_____
4. Who / your best friend five years ago ? _____
_____
5. you / ever move when you were a child ? _____
_____
6. you / play outside a lot when you were little ? _____
_____
7. How old / you when you started school ? _____
_____

1 What's the subject?

Vocabulary **A** **Cross out the word that doesn't belong. Then write the general category of the subjects.**

1.	history	~~chemistry~~	economics	geography	*social studies*
2.	gymnastics	dance	art	track	_____
3.	geometry	computer studies	algebra	calculus	_____
4.	literature	biology	chemistry	physics	_____
5.	choir	band	drama	orchestra	_____

B **Complete the crossword puzzle.**

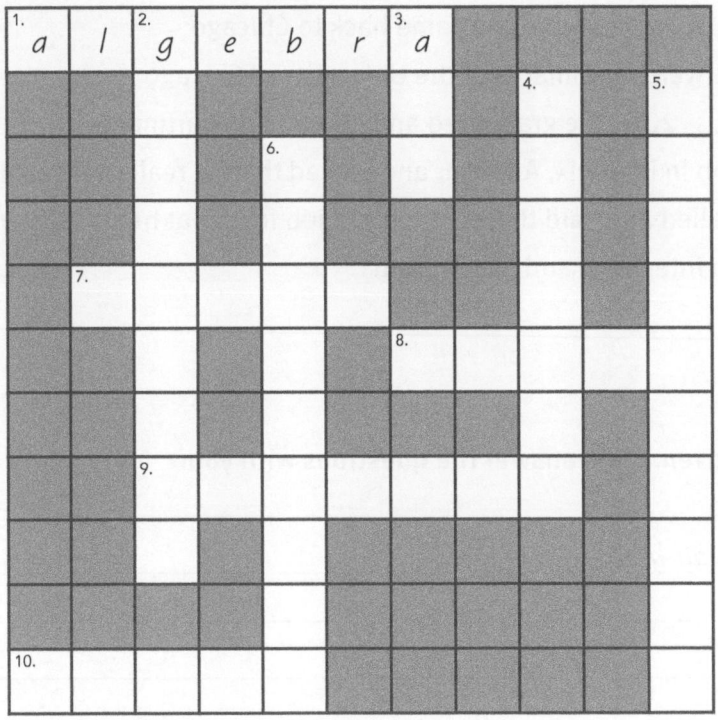

Across

1. This is one subject in math.
7. Students run short and long distances in this P.E. class.
8. Students learn to sing in this music class.
9. In this subject, students study about people and events from a long time ago.
10. Students learn to be actors when they study this subject.

Down

2. In this class, students study countries of the world and natural features, populations, and climate.
3. Students draw and paint in this class.
4. This subject is a science. Students learn about plant and animal life.
5. In this subject, teachers ask students to read novels, stories, and poems.
6. In this class, students play classical music on instruments.

2 How did we do?

Grammar **A Write the determiners in order in the chart below.**

a few ✓all a lot of most none of some

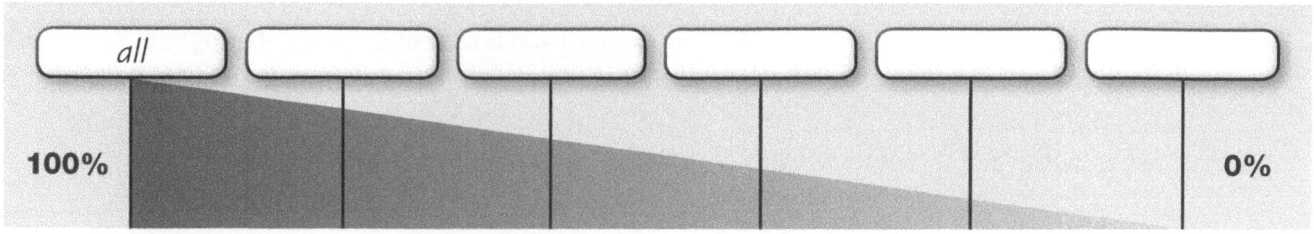

B Read the test results. Then complete the sentences with the words in the box and add *of* where necessary. Some expressions are used more than once.

	A	B	C	D	E
1		**Chemistry**	**English**	**Geography**	**Geometry**
2	**Passed**	55%	100%	90%	15%
3	**Failed**	45%	0%	10%	85%

A few All A lot Most None Some

1. *Some* students in the class passed chemistry. _____ them failed chemistry.
2. _____ the students passed English. _____ the students failed it.
3. _____ the students passed geography. _____ students failed it.
4. _____ students passed geometry. _____ them failed it.

3 About you

Grammar and vocabulary **Answer the questions with your own information. If you are still in high school, write about last year.**

When you were in high school, what was a subject . . .

1. most of your friends liked? *Most of my friends liked P.E.*
2. all of the students had to study? _____
3. a lot of students hated? _____
4. some of your classmates loved? _____
5. no students ever failed? _____
6. a few students were always really good at? _____
7. none of your classmates liked? _____
8. a lot of students got good grades in? _____
9. some students dropped? _____

1 Correcting things you say

Conversation strategies **Complete the conversations with the sentences in the box.**

Actually, no, it was 2009.	Actually, I guess I spent some weekends with my grandparents.
Well, at least most of them didn't.	Well, actually, we had a few problems. My dad lost his job.
No, wait. I was nine.	✓Well, not all of them. Josie speaks three languages.
Well, actually, it was dark brown.	No, wait. . . . Her name was Mrs. Santos.
Actually, no, I was 18 when I quit.	

1. A All my friends are bilingual. They all speak two languages.
   Well, not all of them. Josie speaks three languages.
   B That's amazing!

2. A My best friend and I had sleepovers every weekend when we were kids.
   _____
   B That sounds like fun.

3. A We moved to Rio de Janeiro when I was ten.
   _____
   B So you were pretty young.

4. A I was on a swimming team until I was 16.
   _____
   B That's the reason you swim so well.

5. A My brother and I had a perfect childhood.
   _____
   B Really? But you were generally pretty happy, right?

6. A My cousin lived with us for a year – in 2010, I think.
   _____
   B That was your cousin Alice, right?

7. A My favorite teacher in elementary school was Mrs. Santana.
   _____
   B Oh, yeah? My favorite teacher was Mr. Stiller.

8. A When I was little, none of my friends had pets.
   _____
   B But you had a dog, right?

9. A I had black hair when I was born.
   _____
   B Really? I was born with no hair at all!

2 I mean

Conversation strategies **Complete the questions using *I mean* to correct the underlined words. Then answer the questions.**

1. When you were a child, what was the name of your first professor, *I mean, teacher* ?

   _____

2. Were you six or seven when you started high school, _____ ?

   _____

3. In elementary school, did you have lunch in the school gym, _____ ?

   _____

4. When you were young, what was your favorite sport, _____ ?
   Did you like checkers? _____

5. When you were young, did you play any music, _____ , like the piano?

   _____

3 About you

Conversation strategies **Complete these sentences so they are true for you.**

1. I started school when I was three. Actually, no,
   when I was five _____ .
2. The name of my elementary school was Park Elementary.
   No, wait. . . . _____ .
3. My first teacher's name was Miss Parker, I mean,
   _____ .
4. I got good grades in every subject. Well, _____
   _____ .
5. Most of my childhood friends liked classical music. Well,
   no, _____ .
6. When I was a child, my favorite holiday was Halloween, I
   mean, _____ .
7. I remember all my classmates in kindergarten. Well, actually, _____ .
8. A lot of my friends did gymnastics or played sports after school.
   No, wait. . . . _____ .
9. We always had pizza for school lunch.
   Well, actually, _____ .

1 Small-town story

Reading **A Read the story of Yolanda's life. Then number the pictures in the correct order.**

Interview: A happy childhood by Kathy Montaño

Kathy Montaño grew up in the small town of Bagdad, Arizona. She interviewed several Mexican Americans in Bagdad about their childhood. This is the story of Yolanda Sandoval.

"My name is Yolanda Sandoval. I was born in Cananea, Mexico, on June 13, 1922. My parents brought me to Bagdad when I was six months old. My father's name was Francisco Sandoval, and my mother's name was Cecilia Bernal.

I was their first child. I have four younger brothers. My mother gave Rafael, my third brother, her name as a middle name. Apart from Rafael, no one had a middle name. My mother was very gentle and patient.

My father was very kind but strict. He worked in a mine. He didn't talk much about his work, maybe because he didn't like it. My mother didn't go out to work. She stayed home to take care of us.

My mother always did special things for our birthdays. One year she gave me a purple party. Everything was purple, even the drinks! She also made me a purple dress. That was the best party I ever had. I invited all my friends – except for Bobby. I was angry with him at the time. My mother died when I was 16. I still miss her.

My brothers and I loved the movies. We thought they were wonderful. A man named Angel Ruiz showed old cowboy movies at the local theater, and we went to all of them. He charged five cents for a movie. Sometimes we didn't have the five cents, but he let us see the movie anyway.

I loved school. I had to study English for four years, science for two (I took chemistry and biology), and a foreign language for two years. I took Spanish, of course! Spanish was easy for me, so I got good grades. I also studied U.S. history, home economics, and physical education. I was a good student."

B Read Yolanda's story again. Then complete the sentences.

1. Kathy Montaño interviewed several people in her town about *their childhood*.
2. Yolanda Sandoval came to Bagdad when she _____.
3. Yolanda's father didn't talk much about his work because _____.
4. On Yolanda's birthday one year, her mother gave her _____.
5. At the local movie theater, Yolanda and her brothers saw _____.
6. Yolanda studied English for _____.

2 When I was a teenager

Writing **A Answer these questions about your first year in high school. If you are still in high school, talk about last year. Use *except (for)* or *apart from*.**

1. Did you like your teachers?
   I liked all my teachers except for my history teacher, Mr. Crown.
2. Did you enjoy all your subjects?
   _____
3. Did you get along with all your classmates?
   _____
4. Did you and your best friend do a lot of things together?
   _____

B Write about some of your favorite activities when you were a teenager.

When I was a teenager, I lived in
My friends and I loved to

Unit 5 Progress chart

	What can you do? Mark the boxes. ✓ = I can . . . ? = I need to review how to . . .	To review, go back to these pages in the Student's Book.
Grammar	☐ make statements and ask questions with the simple past and past of *be*.	44 and 45
	☐ talk about the past using time expressions.	44 and 45
	☐ use determiners: *all (of), most (of), a lot of, some (of), a few (of), no, none of.*	46 and 47
Vocabulary	☐ say years.	45
	☐ name at least 12 school subjects.	47
	☐ name at least 5 general subject categories.	47
Conversation strategies	☐ correct things I say with expressions like *Actually* and *No, wait.*	48 and 49
	☐ use *I mean* to correct myself.	49
Writing	☐ use *except (for)* and *apart from* to link ideas.	51

Around town

UNIT 6

Lesson A Finding places

1 Where is it?

Grammar and vocabulary

Look at the map. Write two answers for each question.

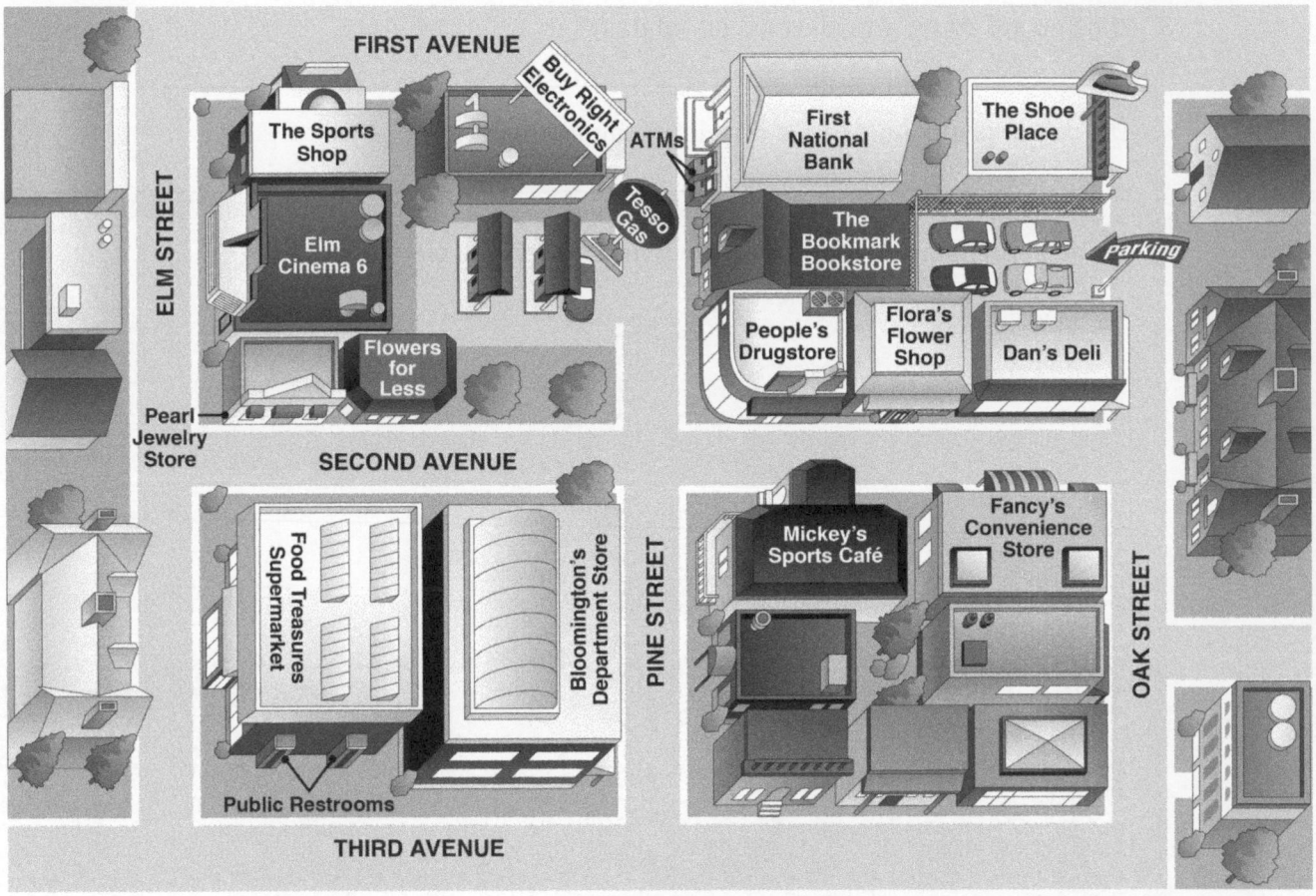

1. Where's the bookstore? *It's on Pine Street, between the bank and the drugstore.*
   It's across the street from the gas station.
2. Where are the public restrooms? _____
3. Where's the parking lot? _____
4. Where are the ATMs? _____
5. Where's the gas station? _____
6. Where's the drugstore? _____

2 Looking for places

Grammar **Write questions. Then complete the answers with *there's one*, *there are some*, *there isn't one*, or *there aren't any*.**

1. A *Is there a drugstore around here?*
   (drugstore around here ?)
   B Yes, *there's one* on the corner of Pine Street and Second Avenue.

2. A _____
   (parking lot near here ?)
   B _____ on Oak Street, behind the bookstore.

3. A _____
   (ATMs anywhere ?)
   B _____ over there, across from the gas station.

4. A _____
   (museum in this town ?)
   B No, sorry, _____.

5. A _____
   (outdoor cafés near here ?)
   B No, _____ outdoor cafés near here, but there are some restaurants inside the department store on Pine Street.

6. A _____
   (public restrooms around here ?)
   B Yeah, sure, _____ on Third Avenue.

3 About you

Grammar and vocabulary **Write questions. Then answer the questions about your neighborhood.**

1. A (a good coffee shop) *Is there a good coffee shop in this neighborhood?*
   B *Yes, there is. There's Emily's on the corner of Center Avenue and First Street.*

2. A (a big department store) _____
   B _____

3. A (any unusual stores) _____
   B _____

4. A (a convenience store) _____
   B _____

5. A (any cheap restaurants) _____
   B _____

6. A (any ATMs) _____
   B _____

1 Places in town

Vocabulary **Complete the sentences with the places in the box.**

aquarium	museum	running path	stadium	Visitor's Center
✓hotel	parking garage	skateboard ramp	theater	water park

You can . . .

1. sleep at a *hotel* .
2. see sea animals at an _____ .
3. go jogging on a _____ .
4. go skateboarding on a _____ .
5. see a play at a _____ .
6. see art and interesting exhibits at a _____ .
7. ask for information at a _____ .
8. leave your car at a _____ .
9. watch a baseball game at a _____ .
10. swim in an outdoor pool at a _____ .

2 Where am I going?

Vocabulary **Some people are at the Sea View Hotel. Where do they want to go? Look at the map. Complete the conversations with the names of the places.**

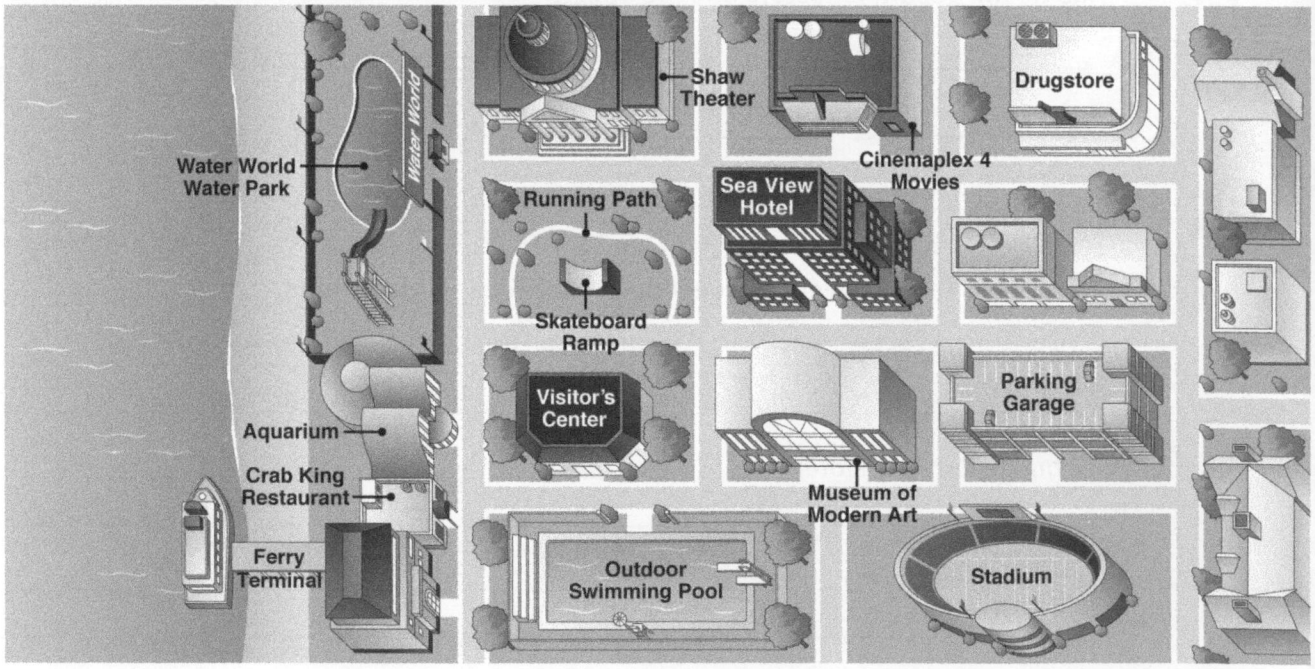

1. A Can you tell me how to get to the _____ ?
   B Sure. When you leave the hotel, turn right. It's on the next block. It's there on your right.
2. A Can you tell me how to get to the _____ ?
   B Yes. Go out of the hotel and turn left. Turn left again at the corner, go one block, and turn right. It's on your left.
3. A Can you help me? I'd like to go to the _____ .
   B Yes. Turn right out of the hotel. Go straight for another block and make a left. Walk two blocks. It's on your right, next to the restaurant.

3 Directions, directions

Grammar and vocabulary

Rewrite the sentences to make requests. Then look at the map on page 44 and write directions.

1. You're at the Visitor's Center. "Tell me how to get to the theater." (Could)
   A *Could you tell me how to get to the theater?*
   B *Sure. Turn right. Then take the first right. Walk straight ahead for two blocks. The theater is going to be there across the street on your right.*

2. You're at the aquarium. "Give me directions to the hotel." (Could)
   A _____
   B _____

3. You're at the aquarium. "Tell me how to get to the drugstore." (Can)
   A _____
   B _____

4. You're at the pool. "How do I get to the stadium?" (Can)
   A _____
   B _____

5. You're at the skateboard ramp. "Give me directions to the ferry terminal." (Could)
   A _____
   B _____

6. You're at the theater. "Tell me how to get to the parking garage." (Can)
   A _____
   B _____

4 About you

Grammar and vocabulary

Complete the offers and requests using *Can* or *Could*. Then answer the questions with true information about the neighborhood you are in now.

1. A _____ recommend a nice restaurant around here?
   B _____

2. A Excuse me. I need some help. _____ help me?
   B Sure. How _____?
   A _____ get to the nearest hotel?
   B _____

3. A _____ directions to a park or a place to go running?
   B _____

1 Checking information

Conversation strategies **Complete the conversations. Check the information.**

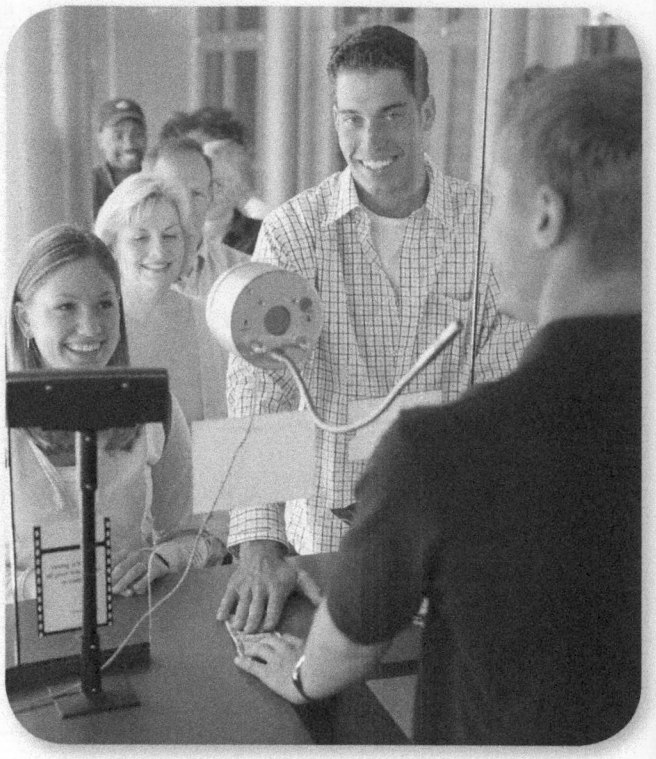

1. A Hi. Where to?
   B I'm going to 830 Center Street.
   A *I'm sorry? Did you say 813 Center Street?*
   B No, 830. That's on the corner of Center and Main – on the left side of the street.
   A _____
   B Yes, the left side.

2. A Could you tell me how to get to Atlantic Bank?
   B _____
   A Yes. Do you know it?
   B I think so. Go straight ahead for three blocks and turn left. It's on the right.
   A _____
   B No. Not on the left. It's on the right.

3. A Can I help you?
   B Yes, please. What time does the next show start?
   A At 7:15.
   B _____
   A 7:15.
   B And what time does it end?
   A It ends at 9:05.
   B _____
   A Yes, that's right.

4. A Can you give me directions to a pet store?
   B _____
   A No, not a bookstore – a pet store. I want to buy some new fish for my aquarium.
   B Oh. Let me think. I think there's a pet store at Bay Street Mall.
   A _____
   B Bay Street Mall. It's about half an hour from here.

2 I'm sorry?

Conversation strategies

Complete the "echo" questions with the words in the box. Use each one only once. There are two extra.

how much	what	what kind	what time	when	where

1. A A new deli opened right across the street from us.
   B I'm sorry, a new _____ opened?
   A A new deli. Let's try it. Then you don't need to cook!

2. A My brother spent almost five hundred dollars on theater tickets for his family.
   B Sorry? He spent _____ ?
   A Almost five hundred dollars. I hope it's a good show!

3. A I really want to leave at 6:00.
   B Sorry? You want to leave at _____ ?
   A At 6:00. Oh, it's already ten after. We're late!

4. A Did you remember? We're going to the aquarium today.
   B I'm sorry? We're going _____ ?
   A To the aquarium. Did you forget?

3 Questions, questions

Conversation strategies

Complete the conversations with "echo" questions.

1. A Do you have your wallet? The tickets are 60 dollars each.
   B They cost *how much?*
   A Sixty dollars each. Hurry. The show starts in 15 minutes. At 3:00.
   B At _____ ?
   A At three. Hurry! It's going to be fun. There are going to be acrobats and things.
   B There are going to be _____ ?
   Um, maybe we should just go to a movie instead!

2. A Let's go to the park today. There's a new bike path.
   B A new _____ ?
   A A bike path. We can go cycling. And then we can go to Primm's.
   B We can go _____ ?
   A Primm's. It's an ice cream place near the park. It sells really good pistachio ice cream.
   B Um, OK. But wait, it sells _____ of ice cream?

1 Life down under

Reading **A Read the article about Coober Pedy. Check (✓) the items the article talks about.**

- ☐ an amusement park
- ☐ an underground hotel
- ☐ a rock and roll museum
- ☐ a place that looks like the moon
- ☐ a drive-in movie theater
- ☐ an opal mine

Coober Pedy

COOBER PEDY
—THE OPAL CAPITAL OF THE WORLD

Welcome to the desert town of Coober Pedy in the outback of Australia. The name Coober Pedy comes from the Aboriginal words *kupa piti*, which mean "white man in a hole." We hope you'll come visit.

Explorers first found opals in this area on February 1, 1915. In 1946, an Aboriginal woman named Tottie Bryant dug out a large and valuable opal. After that, a lot of people came to Coober Pedy to mine opals.

During the 1960s, many European immigrants came to work here, and Coober Pedy quickly became a large modern town. Today, Coober Pedy is the world's main source of high-quality opals and a unique tourist spot.

It's so hot in Coober Pedy that a lot of people live underground! There are many underground homes, as well as underground hotels, museums, opal shops, art galleries, and, of course, opal mines.

Here are some places to visit during your stay.

Umoona Opal Mine & Museum is a unique underground museum about the history of the town. It includes a model underground home and a small opal mine. Some of the world's finest opals are on display here.

The Moon Plain is a large rocky area unlike anywhere else. It looks like the moon – or another planet! It was the set for many movies, including *Mad Max Beyond Thunderdome, The Adventures of Priscilla, Queen of the Desert,* and *The Red Planet*. It is about 15 kilometers northeast of Coober Pedy.

Coober Pedy Drive-In is an open-air movie theater. You can see a movie there every other Saturday night.

B Read the article again. Then match the two parts of each sentence.

1. The name Coober Pedy means __d__
2. Tottie Bryant found ____
3. Coober Pedy became a modern mining town when ____
4. Right now, Coober Pedy is the world's main source ____
5. As a tourist place, Coober Pedy is famous for ____
6. The Moon Plain was ____

a. the set for many movies.
b. a very big and valuable opal.
c. its underground homes, museums, stores, and mines.
✓d. "white man in a hole."
e. immigrants came to work in the mines.
f. of high-quality opals.

2 Walking guide

Writing **A Read this New Orleans walking tour. Look at the map and fill in the missing words.**

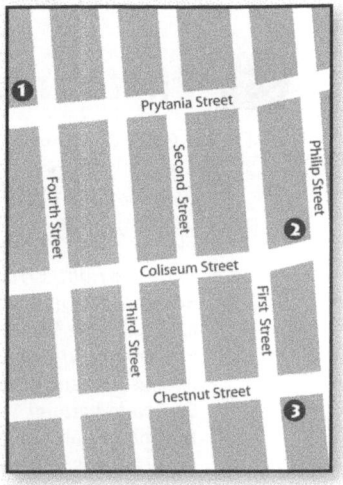

1. This is the Garden District Book Shop. Anne Rice, a famous author from New Orleans, calls this her favorite bookstore.
2. Take Prytania Street ___*four*___ blocks to Philip Street. Turn _____ on Philip Street. Take Philip Street one _____ to Coliseum Street. _____ a right on Coliseum Street. The homes on the _____ are called the Seven Sisters. A man wanted his seven daughters to live close to him. He built these seven houses for them as wedding gifts.
3. Go _____ on Coliseum Street and walk to the end of the block. _____ left on First Street. Go _____ for one block. It's right there, on the _____ . This is the Brevard-Mahat-Rice House, where Anne Rice lives and works.

B Think of two tourist attractions in your town or city. Write directions from one to the other.

Start at

Unit 6 Progress chart

What can you do? Mark the boxes. ✓ = I can . . . ? = I need to review how to . . .	To review, go back to these pages in the Student's Book.
Grammar	
☐ use *Is there?* and *Are there?* to ask about places in a town.	54 and 55
☐ use *across from, behind, between*, etc., to describe location.	55
☐ make offers and requests with *Can* and *Could*.	56 and 57
Vocabulary	
☐ name at least 15 places in a city or town.	54, 55, and 56
Conversation strategies	
☐ check information by repeating key words and using "checking" expressions.	58 and 59
☐ ask "echo" questions to check information.	59
Writing	
☐ write a guide giving directions.	61

Illustration credits

Ken Batelman: 42, 44 **Lisa Blackshear:** 24 **Domninic Bugatto:** 14, 34, 82, 83 **Cambridge University Press:** 25, 27, 49, 52 **Daniel Chen:** 6, 94 **Matt Collins:** 40 **Chuck Gonzales:** 19, 29, 67, 75, 85, 96 **Frank Montagna:** 10, 22, 30, 58, 59, 69, 78 **Marilena Perilli:** 5, 66, 70, 85 **Greg White:** 20, 47, 62, 63, 91 **Terry Wong:** 2, 3, 28, 55, 61

Photo credits

4 *(clockwise from top left)* ©JupiterImages; ©Monkey Business Images/Shutterstock; ©Alan Thornton/Getty Images; ©YURI KADOBNOV/AFP/Getty Images; ©Ocean/Corbis; ©Punchstock **8** ©Kjpargeter/Shutterstock **11** ©Image Source/SuperStock **12** *(top row, left to right)* ©Henry Diltz/Corbis; ©Charles Sykes/Associated Press; ©Matt Kent/WireImage/Getty Images; ©Frank Micelotta/Getty Images *(top row, left to right)* ©Barros & Barros/Getty Images; ©Tim Mosenfelder/Corbis; ©Al Bello/Getty Images; ©Peter Kramer/NBC/NBCU Photo Bank via Getty Images **13** *(top to bottom)* ©Jason Merritt/Getty Images For BET; ©Jon Kopaloff/FilmMagic/Getty Images **15** *(left to right)* ©Thinkstock; ©Sebastien Starr/Getty Images **16** *(background)* ©tdixon8875/Shutterstock **18** *(top to bottom)* ©Image Source/Getty Images; ©Digital Vision/Getty Images **21** *(clockwise from top left)* ©Mary Kate Denny/PhotoEdit; ©Dana White/PhotoEdit; ©Thinkstock; ©Jose Luis Pelaez Inc./Corbis **25** ©Punchstock **26** *(top to bottom)* ©Gregg DeGuire/WireImage/Getty Images; ©Russ Einhorn 2004/Russ Einhorn/Splash News/Newscom; ©Jason LaVeris/FilmMagic/Getty Images; ©Gregg DeGuire/WireImage/Getty Images; ©Jason LaVeris/FilmMagic/Getty Images; ©Alex Livesey - FIFA/FIFA via Getty Images **31** ©Keren Su/China Span/Alamy **32** *(top to bottom)* ©Anna-Mari West/Shutterstock; ©Africa Studio/Shutterstock **35** ©Michael Newman/PhotoEdit **39** ©Michael Newman/PhotoEdit **46** *(left to right)* ©Blend Images/SuperStock; ©Andersen Ross/Getty Images **48** *(top to bottom)* ©Joel Arem/Getty Images; ©HUGHES Herve/hemis.fr/Getty Images; ©Andrew Watson/Getty Images **50** ©Ralph Lee Hopkins/Getty Images **51** ©Dave Fleetham/Pacific Stock - Design Pics/SuperStock *(background)* ©sdecoret/Shutterstock **53** *(left to right)* ©Thinkstock; ©Jupiterimages/Thinkstock **54** *(top to bottom)* ©Greg Elms/Getty Images; ©Michael Goldman/Masterfile **56** *(left to right)* ©Purcell Team/Alamy; ©DIOMEDIA/Alamy; ©Peter Grant/Getty Images **57** ©Trish Punch/Getty Images **64** Photos Courtesy of Poezenboot **68** *(top to bottom)* ©Thinkstock; ©Punchstock **76** *(left to right)* ©PhotoInc/Getty Images; ©Kablonk/SuperStock **77** ©Dougal Waters/Getty Images **80** ©Raoul Minsart/Masterfile *(background)* ©Kjpargeter/Shutterstock **82** ©David Lees/Getty Images **84** *(top to bottom)* ©Punchstock; ©largeformat4x5/Getty Images; ©Seth Resnick/Science Faction/SuperStock **86** *(top to bottom)* ©Maximiliano Failla/AFP/Getty Images; ©Shaun Botterill - FIFA/FIFA via Getty Images; ©STR/AFP/Getty Images; ©s_bukley/Shutterstock **87** *(top to bottom)* ©David Cannon/Getty Images; ©Ric Francis/Associated Press; ©DFree/Shutterstock; ©cinemafestival/Shutterstock; ©Clive Brunskill/Getty Images; ©Elnur/Shutterstock; ©Amos Morgan/Thinkstock; ©Thinkstock; ©Jupiterimages/Thinkstock **88** *(left to right)* ©imagebroker.net/SuperStock; ©Iain McKell/Getty Images; ©Masterfile; ©Nick Dolding/Getty Images; ©Ellen Stagg/Getty Images; ©Thinkstock *(background)* ©alex.makarova/Shutterstock **92** *(left column, top to bottom)* ©Punchstock; ©George Doyle/Thinkstock; ©George Doyle & Ciaran Griffin/Thinkstock; ©Jack Hollingsworth/Getty Images; ©Corbis; ©Thinkstock *(middle column, top to bottom)* ©Jupiterimages/Thinkstock; ©Thinkstock; ©Jeff Greenberg/PhotoEdit; ©David Young-Wolff/PhotoEdit; ©Michael Newman/PhotoEdit; ©Tetra Images/Getty Images *(right column, top to bottom)* ©Tom Carter/PhotoEdit; ©Jupiterimages/Thinkstock; ©Thinkstock; ©Flying Colours Ltd/Getty Images; ©Robin Nelson/PhotoEdit; ©JupiterImages

Text credits

While every effort has been made, it has not always been possible to identify the sources of all the material used, or to trace all copyright holders. If any omissions are brought to our notice, we will be happy to include the appropriate acknowledgements on reprinting.

The top 500 spoken words

This is a list of the top 500 words in spoken North American English. It is based on a sample of four and a half million words of conversation from the Cambridge International Corpus. The most frequent word, *I*, is at the top of the list.

1. I
2. and
3. the
4. you
5. uh
6. to
7. a
8. that
9. it
10. of
11. yeah
12. know
13. in
14. like
15. they
16. have
17. so
18. was
19. but
20. is
21. it's
22. we
23. huh
24. just
25. oh
26. do
27. don't
28. that's
29. well
30. for
31. what
32. on
33. think
34. right
35. not
36. um
37. or
38. my
39. be
40. really
41. with
42. he
43. one
44. are
45. this
46. there
47. I'm
48. all
49. if
50. no
51. get
52. about
53. at
54. out
55. had
56. then
57. because
58. go
59. up
60. she
61. when
62. them
63. can
64. would
65. as
66. me
67. mean
68. some
69. good
70. got
71. OK
72. people
73. now
74. going
75. were
76. lot
77. your
78. time
79. see
80. how
81. they're
82. kind
83. here
84. from
85. did
86. something
87. too
88. more
89. very
90. want
91. little
92. been
93. things
94. an
95. you're
96. said
97. there's
98. I've
99. much
100. where
101. two
102. thing
103. her
104. didn't
105. other
106. say
107. back
108. could
109. their
110. our
111. guess
112. yes
113. way
114. has
115. down
116. we're
117. any

118. he's
119. work
120. take
121. even
122. those
123. over
124. probably
125. him
126. who
127. put
128. years
129. sure
130. can't
131. pretty
132. gonna
133. stuff
134. come
135. these
136. by
137. into
138. went
139. make
140. than
141. year
142. three
143. which
144. home
145. will
146. nice
147. never
148. only
149. his
150. doing
151. cause
152. off
153. I'll
154. maybe
155. real
156. why
157. big
158. actually
159. she's
160. day
161. five
162. always
163. school
164. look
165. still
166. around
167. anything
168. kids
169. first
170. does
171. need
172. us
173. should
174. talking
175. last
176. thought
177. doesn't
178. different
179. money
180. long
181. used
182. getting
183. same
184. four
185. every
186. new
187. everything
188. many
189. before
190. though
191. most
192. tell
193. being
194. bit
195. house
196. also
197. use
198. through
199. feel
200. course
201. what's
202. old
203. done
204. sort
205. great
206. bad
207. we've
208. another
209. car
210. true
211. whole
212. whatever
213. twenty
214. after
215. ever
216. find
217. care
218. better
219. hard
220. haven't
221. trying
222. give
223. I'd
224. problem
225. else
226. remember
227. might
228. again
229. pay
230. try
231. place
232. part
233. let
234. keep
235. children
236. anyway
237. came
238. six
239. family
240. wasn't
241. talk
242. made
243. hundred
244. night
245. call
246. saying

247. dollars
248. live
249. away
250. either
251. read
252. having
253. far
254. watch
255. week
256. mhm
257. quite
258. enough
259. next
260. couple
261. own
262. wouldn't
263. ten
264. interesting
265. am
266. sometimes
267. bye
268. seems
269. heard
270. goes
271. called
272. point
273. ago
274. while
275. fact
276. once
277. seen
278. wanted
279. isn't
280. start
281. high
282. somebody
283. let's
284. times
285. guy
286. area
287. fun
288. they've
289. you've
290. started
291. job
292. says
293. play
294. usually
295. wow
296. exactly
297. took
298. few
299. child
300. thirty
301. buy
302. person
303. working
304. half
305. looking
306. someone
307. coming
308. eight
309. love
310. everybody
311. able
312. we'll
313. life
314. may
315. both
316. type
317. end
318. least
319. told
320. saw
321. college
322. ones
323. almost
324. since
325. days
326. couldn't
327. gets
328. guys
329. god
330. country
331. wait
332. yet
333. believe
334. thinking
335. funny
336. state
337. until
338. husband
339. idea
340. name
341. seven
342. together
343. each
344. hear
345. help
346. nothing
347. parents
348. room
349. today
350. makes
351. stay
352. mom
353. sounds
354. change
355. understand
356. such
357. gone
358. system
359. comes
360. thank
361. show
362. thousand
363. left
364. friends
365. class
366. already
367. eat
368. small
369. boy
370. paper
371. world
372. best
373. water
374. myself
375. run

376. they'll
377. won't
378. movie
379. cool
380. news
381. number
382. man
383. basically
384. nine
385. enjoy
386. bought
387. whether
388. especially
389. taking
390. sit
391. book
392. fifty
393. months
394. women
395. month
396. found
397. side
398. food
399. looks
400. summer
401. hmm
402. fine
403. hey
404. student
405. agree
406. mother
407. problems
408. city
409. second
410. definitely
411. spend
412. happened
413. hours
414. war
415. matter
416. supposed
417. worked
418. company
419. friend
420. set
421. minutes
422. morning
423. between
424. music
425. close
426. leave
427. wife
428. knew
429. pick
430. important
431. ask
432. hour
433. deal
434. mine
435. reason
436. credit
437. dog
438. group
439. turn
440. making
441. American
442. weeks
443. certain
444. less
445. must
446. dad
447. during
448. lived
449. forty
450. air
451. government
452. eighty
453. wonderful
454. seem
455. wrong
456. young
457. places
458. girl
459. happen
460. sorry
461. living
462. drive
463. outside
464. bring
465. easy
466. stop
467. percent
468. hand
469. gosh
470. top
471. cut
472. computer
473. tried
474. gotten
475. mind
476. business
477. anybody
478. takes
479. aren't
480. question
481. rather
482. twelve
483. phone
484. program
485. without
486. moved
487. gave
488. yep
489. case
490. looked
491. certainly
492. talked
493. beautiful
494. card
495. walk
496. married
497. anymore
498. you'll
499. middle
500. tax